FOXES

AND THEIR HOMES

Deborah Chase Gibson

The Rosen Publishing Group's
PowerKids Press™
New York

Published in 1999 by The Rosen Publishing Group, Inc.
29 East 21st Street, New York, NY 10010

First Edition

Book Design: Kim Sonsky

Photo Credits: Cover, Title page, p. 15 © Johnny Johnson/Animals Animals; Contents page © Joe McDonald/Animals Animals; p. 4 © Gail Shumway/FPG International; p. 5 © Susan Pfannmuller/Midwest Stock; p. 7 © Breck P. Kent/Animals Animals; p. 8 © Mella Panzella/Animals Animals; pp. 11, Back Cover © Darek Karp/Animals Animals; p. 12 © Scott WM. Hanrahan/ International Stock; p. 16 © Bob Jacobson/International Stock; p. 18 © Richard Kolar/Animals Animals; p. 21 © 1996 PhotoDisc, Inc.; p. 22 © Jeffrey Sylvester/FPG International; p. 24 © Victoria McCormick/Animals Animals.

Gibson, Deborah Chase.
    Foxes and their homes / Deborah Chase Gibson.
        p. cm. — (Animal Habitats)
    Includes index.
    Summary: Presents an overview of different kinds of foxes and how and where they make their homes.
    ISBN 0-8239-5309-2
    1. Foxes—Juvenile literature. 2. Foxes—Habitat—Juvenile literature. [1. Foxes.] I. Title. II. Series:
Gibson, Deborah Chase. Animal habitats.
    QL737.C22G53   1998
    599.775—dc21   98-15384
                                                                                              CIP
                                                                                               AC

Manufactured in the United States of America

CONTENTS

1 Foxes of the World   4
2 What Are Red Foxes Like?   6
3 Finding a Den   9
4 Inside the Den   10
5 A Family of Foxes   13
6 The Arctic   14
7 The Arctic Fox   17
8 The Desert Fox   19
9 Foxhunting   20
10 Foxes and Humans   22
   Web Sites   22
   Glossary   23
   Index   24

FOXES OF THE WORLD

Foxes are found in many different **habitats** (HA-bih-tats), from deserts to mountains to forests to the icy Arctic. Some foxes even live near cities. There are fox habitats all over the northern part of the world, as well as in Africa and Australia. Several close cousins of the fox live in South America.

Foxes belong to the same animal family as dogs, coyotes, jackals, and wolves. There are a number of **species** (SPEE-sheez), or kinds, of foxes. This means that all foxes look alike in certain ways. But they are also different in other ways, such as the color of their fur or where their habitat is.

Foxes look a lot like dogs because both species are part of the dog family. ▶

◀ Unlike wild dogs, foxes, such as this Arctic fox, do not hunt for food in packs, or groups.

WHAT ARE RED FOXES LIKE?

When most people think of a fox, they picture a red fox. This fox lives in North America, Europe, Asia, Australia, and parts of Africa. Red foxes aren't always red. Like other kinds of foxes, they can be silver, black, tan, or orange. Their thick, fluffy coats and long tails make their bodies seem bigger than they really are. Most foxes are only two to three feet long from their noses to their tails. They are a little more than one foot tall. Red foxes hunt and eat rabbits, small birds, mice, and **voles** (VOHLZ). In fact, red foxes are such good hunters that Europeans brought them to Australia in the 1800s to help control the number of rabbits that lived there.

Most red foxes weigh about fifteen pounds. ▶

FINDING A DEN

When foxes are ready to **mate** (MAYT) and have babies, or pups, they search their habitat for a **den** (DEN). Foxes need the safety of a den as they give birth to their pups and raise them. But foxes don't like to dig their own dens. They try to find dens that are already made. They will often search for **burrows** (BUR-ohz) left by other animals, such as prairie dogs, porcupines, or woodchucks.

Once they find a good den, the male and female fox make it into a home. They clean the den and make it larger with more digging.

A fox that doesn't have pups usually won't live in a den. ◀ This kit fox might simply climb to a safe place, such as a ledge, to sleep.

INSIDE THE DEN

Some fox dens have a few holes through which foxes can enter. These holes in the ground lead to tunnels that open up to big spaces inside the den. Females give birth to their pups in these rooms. Mothers **nurse** (NURS) their helpless pups until the pups are old enough to move around by themselves.

A den is an important gathering place for a family of foxes. Foxes keep their dens very clean. A den **shelters** (SHEL-turz) young foxes from the weather and from **predators** (PREH-duh-terz), such as bears or coyotes. As adults, foxes don't need dens for shelter. They can **survive** (sur-VYV) above the ground.

These red fox pups are safe in their den, which is also called an earth. ▶

A FAMILY OF FOXES

Female foxes give birth to three to five pups at one time. When pups are born, they can't see or walk. So their mother stays in the den to take care of them. She feeds the pups milk from her body. This is the way dogs and humans feed their babies. The father fox hunts outside the den. He brings food to the mother so that she won't have to leave the pups.

Soon the pups grow stronger. They are able to leave the den. They learn to hunt and play with each other. Five to ten months after they're born, the pups have grown into adults. They are ready to find their own mates.

◀ These red fox pups first learn how to hunt by playing with each other.

THE ARCTIC

The icy, cold Arctic lies at the top of the world. The northern parts of Alaska, Canada, Europe, and Siberia lie in and near the Arctic Circle. The land in the Arctic is called **tundra** (TUN-druh). It is so cold in this part of the world that the top six inches of the land are frozen solid.

This cold **climate** (KLY-mit) is the habitat of the Arctic fox. It is very hard to dig a den in the frozen tundra. So Arctic foxes make their dens in mounds of earth above the ground. Sometimes they make dens inside piles of rock or under pieces of wood.

These Arctic fox pups have dark fur because it is summer. Their color helps them blend in ▶ with the entrance to their den.

THE ARCTIC FOX

   The winter coats of Arctic foxes are white with bits of gray, or bluish gray. Their fluffy, thick coats protect them from the icy weather. Like the red fox, Arctic foxes **molt** (MOHLT) in the spring. That means they shed their heavy winter coats to get ready for warm weather. In the summer, their coats turn darker. This helps Arctic foxes blend in with their habitat.

   When Arctic foxes are not in their dens raising pups, they are out hunting for food. These foxes often spend many months on the ice that covers parts of the Arctic Ocean. Sometimes they follow polar bears around and eat their leftovers.

◀ Arctic foxes have soft, thick fur that keeps them warm on the tundra. Their coats turn white in the winter so they can blend in with the snow.

17

The kit fox has large ears that let its body heat escape. This helps it keep cool.

THE DESERT FOX

While the Arctic fox lives in the coldest place on Earth, the kit fox lives in one of the hottest. Deserts, such as those found in the southwestern United States, are the habitats of the kit fox. Deserts are very dry, hot places. Still, lots of plants grow there. And many animals, such as lizards, snakes, and **rodents** (ROH-dents), make their homes in the desert.

During the day, the kit fox rests in a den to avoid the sun and heat. These foxes hunt at night when it isn't as hot. Kit foxes eat crickets, mice, and rabbits. Sometimes they eat the sweet fruit of cactus plants. The kit fox has feet that are lined with fur. This allows it to walk across hot rocks or sand in the desert.

FOXHUNTING

Long ago, humans and animals lived side by side. Humans hunted animals, including foxes, for food and clothing. People no longer need to do this today. Sadly, some people still hunt foxes for sport, or fun. Foxhunting has been a very popular sport in England since the 1500s. Hunters ride on horses and follow a pack of dogs. The dogs chase a fox through its habitat, over open fields and hills. Once the dogs surround it, the hunters kill the fox. If the fox is a father who left his forest den to hunt for food, his mate and pups may **starve** (STARV).

Many people in England are now fighting to stop foxhunting. They want to make it **illegal** (ih-LEE-gul) so that foxes and their habitats are safe.

In England, the red fox is hunted for sport. ▶

FOXES AND HUMANS

Foxes have many enemies, including predators. But their worst enemies are humans. People have taken over many of the forests and lands where foxes make their homes. This makes it harder for foxes to live in peace. A safe home is just as important to foxes as it is to you.

Many foxes have had to leave their natural habitats and find new places to live. Sometimes, they are even forced to live in cities and big towns.

We must protect foxes and their natural habitats. If we work together, we can help keep foxes from ever becoming an **endangered** (en-DAYN-jurd) species.

WEB SITES:

You can learn more about foxes on the Internet. Check out these Web sites:
http://www.vulpes.org/
http://tavi.acomp.usf.edu/foxbox/

GLOSSARY

burrow (BUR-oh) A hole dug in the ground by animals for shelter.

climate (KLY-mit) The kind of weather a certain area has.

den (DEN) An animal's home.

endangered (en-DAYN-jurd) When something is in danger of no longer existing.

habitat (HA-bih-tat) The surroundings where an animal lives.

illegal (ih-LEE-gul) Against the law.

mate (MAYT) A special joining of a male and female body. After mating, the female may have a baby grow inside her body.

molt (MOHLT) When an animal sheds its coat or skin.

nurse (NURS) When a mother gives her milk to her babies.

predator (PREH-duh-ter) An animal that kills other animals for food.

rodent (ROH-dent) A kind of animal, such as a mouse, a rat, or a squirrel.

shelter (SHEL-tur) Something that protects from attacks, danger, and weather.

species (SPEE-sheez) A group of animals that are very much alike.

starve (STARV) To suffer or die from hunger.

survive (sur-VYV) To keep living.

tundra (TUN-druh) The frozen land of the coldest parts of the world.

vole (VOHL) A small mouse-like rodent.

INDEX

A
Arctic fox, 14, 17

B
burrow, 9

C
cactus, 19
cities, 4, 22
climate, 14
coat, 17

D
den, 9, 10, 13, 14, 17, 19, 20
desert, 4, 19
dogs, 4, 13, 20

E
endangered, 22
enemies, 22

F
forest, 4, 20, 22
fur, 5, 19

H
habitat, 4–5, 9, 14, 17, 19, 20, 22
humans, 13, 20, 22
hunting, 6, 13, 17, 19, 20

I
illegal, 20

K
kit fox, 19

M
mate, 9, 13, 20
milk, 13
molt, 17
mountains, 4

N
nurse, 10

P
predators, 10, 22
pups, 9, 10, 13, 17, 20

R
red fox, 6, 17
rodent, 19

S
shelter, 10
species, 4, 22
starve, 20
survive, 10

T
tundra, 14

V
vole, 6